JANE GOODALL'S ANIMAL WORLD

TIGERS

by Ruth Ashby

Scientific Consultant: Peter Jackson

A Byron Preiss Book

ALADDIN BOOKS
MACMILLAN PUBLISHING COMPANY NEW YORK
COLLIER MACMILLAN PUBLISHERS LONDON

◇ Introduction: The Tiger by Jane Goodall

Tyger! Tyger! burning bright
In the forests of the night . . .

I read these lines from the poem by William Blake when I was young. And I read about Shere Khan in Rudyard Kipling's *The Jungle Books*, the great hunter pitted against all other animals, including Mowgli and the rest of the human tribe. Cunning and cruel, but free and oh so beautiful.

I have seen live tigers only in zoos. I cannot, however, bear the thought of them in captivity. This is not necessarily because it is worse for them than for the other big cats, but because I have associated them, since I was a child, with wildness and the untamed forest. I was desperately unhappy when I first saw tigers pacing to and fro in a little cage with iron bars and a cement floor. One of them rubbed his nose against the bars every time he went past the front of his cage. He had rubbed away the skin and had a wound that never healed.

I was working at that zoo at the time, and I shall never forget the Tiger Lady, as we called her. She was Russian, and she said she had a special relationship with tigers. Day after day, she begged to be allowed to go in with the two great cats. Of course, the zoo authorities could not let her into the cage. But it was so obvious that she had a calming effect. Eventually she was allowed to go behind the scenes to the sleeping cages. And it was unbelievable to see how both tigers came to her, and purred, and rubbed their heads against her hand, for all the world like two domestic cats. The world, truly, is full of wonder and magic.

It is only recently that scientists have made careful studies of individual tigers in the wild, gradually piecing together the pattern of their lives. And it has not been easy, because tigers spend so much time in dense vegetation and they do so much of their hunting at night. But how utterly wonderful it would be to see one of these beautiful creatures moving through the undergrowth, lying stretched out in the sun, shaking the drops of water off its magnificent striped coat after an afternoon swim.

One day, perhaps, I shall have the time to visit tiger country. If so, it will be a childhood dream come true.

◇ Contents

◇ Where Do Tigers Live?

Tigers are found in Asia throughout the Indian subcontinent, Southeast Asia, China, Korea, and Russia. They can survive in many different habitats, or environments. Tigers are found in deciduous forests, evergreen forests, swamps, grasslands, and rain forests.

Wherever tigers live, there is usually a lot of thick cover—trees, bushes, and clumps of tall grass. This helps to shade tigers in areas where the sun is especially hot. It also allows them to blend in with their surroundings. To the animals that tigers hunt, tigers' orange and black striped coats have the same patterns of light and dark as the vegetation. This camouflage helps tigers to surprise their prey.

Because tigers are so sensitive to heat, they like to take cooling swims when the temperature rises. Unlike most cats, they love the water and often live near lakes and rivers.

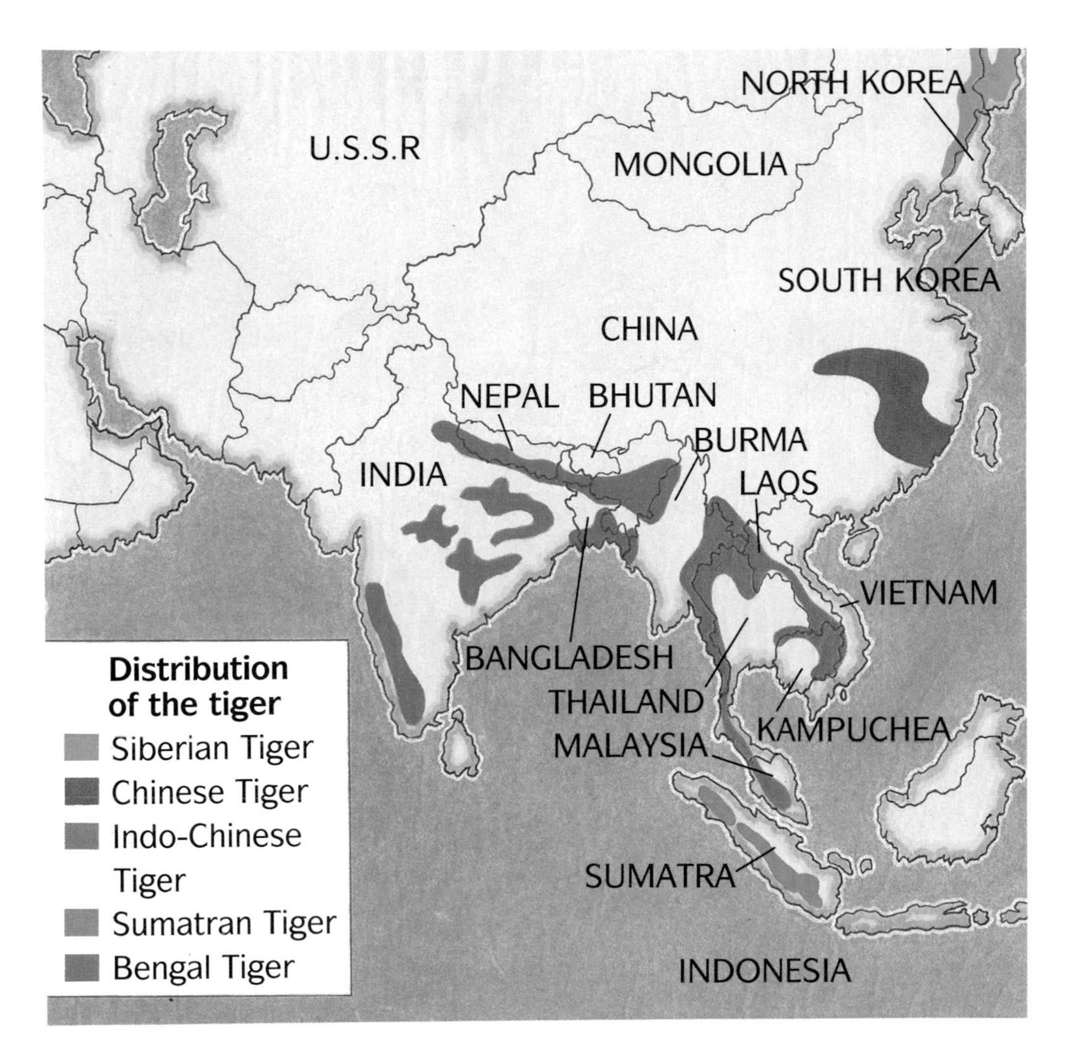

Tigers prey mainly upon grass-eating and other animals, such as deer, buffalo, wild cattle, and wild boars, but they even eat fish and crabs. Other predators also share the tiger's habitat. Depending on where the tiger lives, these can include leopards, wild dogs, crocodiles, and pythons. But adult tigers are so big and powerful that they do not have to worry about competition.

◇ The Family Tree of the Tiger

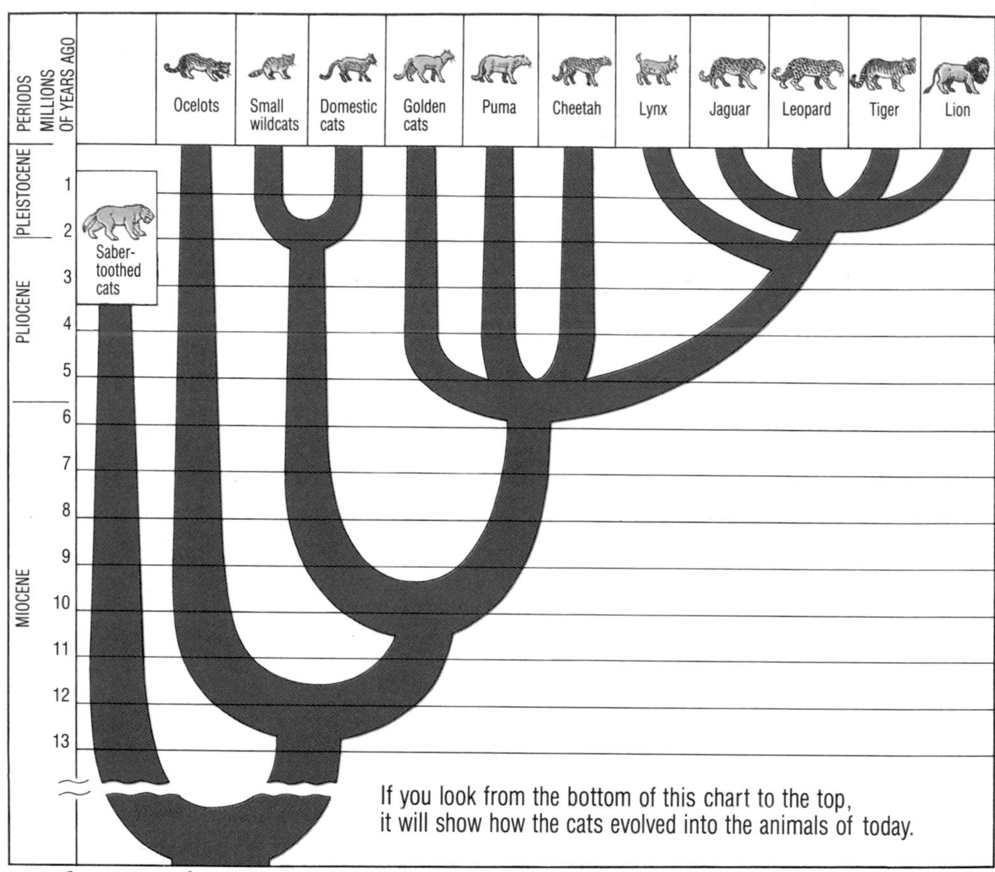

The tiger's scientific name is *Panthera tigris* (pan-*theer*-rah *tee*-gris.) It is a mammal and a member of the cat family. Cats can be divided into two main types, or genera. Big cats, like the tiger, lion, leopard, and jaguar, have parts in their throats that allow them to roar. Small cats, such as the puma, lynx, ocelot, wild cat, and domestic cat, cannot roar. The cheetah belongs to a separate genus of its own.

Once there were eight subspecies of tigers. Today three of them, the Javan tiger, Caspian tiger, and Balinese tiger, are extinct. Only the Indian or Bengal tiger, Indo-Chinese tiger, Chinese tiger, Sumatran tiger, and Siberian tiger still survive. Northern tigers are generally bigger and lighter in color than those in southern climates.

◇ The Tiger Community

Tigers are largely solitary animals. Except when they are cubs, they do not spend their lives in family groups. Related tigers are occasionally seen in friendly meetings. Yet though they are usually alone, each tiger is a part of a larger social organization.

Tigers in the wild inhabit home areas called *ranges*, usually of ten to thirty square miles. The size of the range depends on the availability of prey. The Siberian tiger, whose prey migrates during the year, may have a range as large as 120 square miles. The home range of one adult male will include those of one, two, or more females. Within these ranges, tigers will hunt, mate, and raise their young.

The areas of the ranges themselves are constantly shifting. When one tiger dies or moves away, another tiger will move in to take his or her place. An aging or injured tiger may be driven from its range by a rival. Usually young tigers move out of their mother's range when they become adult. For a while they are wanderers, without a range of their own. When an area becomes vacant, they take it over.

Tigers need all their strength to hunt and kill prey, and rarely

fight among themselves. They mark their ranges with their smell and their dung to let other tigers know it is occupied. This *scent-marking* helps potential rivals keep out of each others' way. It also helps neighbors keep track of each other.

Adult males rarely tolerate the presence of another adult male. They are much more likely to spend time with a female, even when the two aren't mating.

Like other predators, tigers must kill to survive. They hunt alone and depend on their own hunting skills to get enough to eat. Still, they will sometimes share kills. Even when they do, they usually eat one at a time. One tiger will wait until another has finished.

Tigers may hunt at any time, but they are active mainly from late afternoon through the night.

There have been many generalizations about tiger behavior that have been challenged in recent years as tigers in protected reserves have become more visible. Though tigers have been considered solitary, up to nine tigers have been seen sharing one kill. And although male tigers are not known to help the females raise the young, affectionate fathers have been seen playing with their offspring. And so on.

Each tiger is above all an individual, and like all individuals, has its own particular way of behaving.

◇ Sizing Up the Tiger

The tiger and the lion are the two biggest cats. Male tigers are much longer and heavier than females. From nose to tail, males average about nine feet six inches long, and females about eight feet nine inches long. An average adult male tiger weights 400 to 450 pounds and a female about 300 pounds.

The Siberian tiger, the biggest cat of all, can attain a length of twelve feet and a weight of 700 pounds.

◇ How the Tiger Moves

Tigers spend eighty percent of their lives sleeping or resting. When they are active, most of their time is spent patrolling their territories or hunting for prey.

Like other cats, tigers are not built for long-distance running. They cannot outrun most of their quick-footed prey. Instead, they approach possible prey stealthily and then attack in a burst of tremendous power and speed. A hunting tiger will lie concealed in grass or brush for long periods of time. When the prey comes close, the tiger starts to stalk, slowly creeping forward with its belly close to the ground. Finally it bounds forward for the kill.

If the kill is made in an open area, the tiger will drag the carcass to a more sheltered spot. It is so strong it can carry the prey for several miles before it starts to eat.

Tigers are also good, powerful swimmers. When they enter water to cool off, they back in, rear first, and lie down. Tigers will often soak soon after making a kill, especially in hot weather.

◇ The Senses of the Tiger

Like other cats, tigers have excellent eyesight and hearing. Because their eyes are in front of their heads, like those of all hunting animals, they have good depth perception. They can continually refocus their eyes to follow the movements of the animals they hunt. Many grass-eaters, like rabbits or deer, have eyes on the sides of their heads. Their food doesn't move, so they don't need to keep track of how far away it is. But they do need to see predators like the tiger coming from any direction.

Tigers also have a good sense of smell. However, they seem to rely more on sight and sound to locate prey.

◊ How Tigers Communicate

Tigers use their sense of smell to communicate with each other. Both males and females establish their ranges and advertise their presence by scent-marking. Tigers patrolling their ranges will lift their tails and shoot urine onto selected bushes, trees, and grasses. The strong smell of this spray tells other tigers who pass by that this area is "claimed." It also tells them when it was claimed and, often, who claimed it. Neighboring tigers can identify each other by scent, as well as by sight.

Female tigers, or tigresses, who are ready to mate will also use scent-marking to attract a male.

Though ordinarily quiet, tigers can make a variety of sounds. When threatening another, a tiger will often growl or snarl. Females grunt to tell their cubs to follow them. Tigers also roar. Their roar proclaims "I am here!" to the world.

◇ Being Born

When they are between three and four years old, young male and female tigers are ready to mate. The tigress advertises her readiness by repeated scent-markings, roars, and moans. When she attracts a male, they usually spend from three to seven days together. If the tigress becomes pregnant, she gives birth about 93 to 110 days later.

The cubs are born in a secluded place, often a cave or an area of thick bush. There are usually three to four cubs but there can be as many as six or seven in a litter. Blind and helpless at birth, newborn cubs are completely dependent on their mother.

Cubs open their eyes about two weeks later. At first their lives are confined to the den. Not until two to three months have passed do they take their first steps into the world beyond.

◊ Growing Up

Tiger cubs lead dangerous and uncertain lives. Fewer than fifty percent survive past their second year. They are threatened by other predators, such as jackals and hyenas. Even adult male tigers have been known to attack and eat cubs. Sometimes cubs die of disease or injury. When food is scarce, the weakest ones can die from starvation.

Tigresses are caring mothers and do their best to protect their offspring. But when they hunt they must leave their cubs alone for long periods of time.

When her cubs are a few months old, the tigress starts bringing meat back for them to eat. They also continue to drink her milk for about another three months. As the cubs grow, their mother must provide more and more food for them. This is an exhausting time for her. Sometimes she must make a kill every day.

Once they can walk, the cubs start to explore their world. They become familiar with the landmarks of their mother's range. And they play with each other, wrestling, chasing, and

stalking. This play helps them develop their muscles and also gives them practice in the kinds of movements necessary to make a kill.

Tigers are not born knowing how to kill prey. They learn slowly, through trial and error, over a period of years.

Hooved animals are dangerous, and often maim or kill tigers with their hooves or horns. It takes much practice to avoid the hooves and aim for the neck or throat. Young cubs observe their mother at the kill. When they get a bit older, she occasionally brings them an animal she has wounded so that they can kill it themselves. Even when they become expert hunters, tigers make a successful kill only about one in fifteen times.

Male tigers become independent earlier than their sisters and strike out to hunt on their own. But this independence also makes them more vulnerable to injury. This may be one of the reasons that tiger populations in the wild always contain more females than males.

Young tigers finally leave their mothers when they are nearly two years old. Tigers can live up to twenty years.

◇ Living Day to Day

It is dawn in a tiger reserve in northern India. A tigress and her two six-month-old cubs lie sleeping in the thick brush near a huge banyan tree. From the forest canopy above them come the shrieks and calls of peacocks, mynahs, and parakeets welcoming a new day.

The cubs stir, and the male nuzzles his mother and licks her face. All three tigers begin the morning's grooming, licking their bodies with their rough tongues. The tigress gives a huge yawn and grunts at her cubs to follow her.

The three leave their cover and set off for a nearby lake. The

move closer to her, she bursts from her hiding place and bounds toward them. The panicked sambar take off in the opposite direction, giving loud barks of alarm. They all get away. After a brief chase, the tigress gives up and returns to her cubs.

Soon, all go down to the lake, to lie down in the cool water. It is now midmorning, and the sun is hot.

The family spends the remainder of the day resting or sleeping in the shade. Toward late afternoon, the two cubs start to play. They leap into the air, swatting at each other with their paws. One darts into a bush and chases two partridges. They come back to their mother, who licks and nuzzles them

affectionately. After more nudging and jostling, all three fall asleep again.

At dusk, many animals come to the lake to drink. The tigress is hungry and must make a kill. Again she leaves her cubs and waits patiently in the tall grass. This time she is rewarded. A big sambar wanders away from the group. Again she creeps forward, then rushes at him, pounces, and kills him with a bite to the throat. She drags the heavy carcass all the way back to where her cubs are waiting.

The family feeds on and off for the next five hours. When they settle into sleep, the tigress hides the carcass by pawing dirt and grasses over it. The family will rest by the kill for the night. There is plenty of meat for tomorrow, and even the day after.

◇ Tigers in Captivity

Today there are about 1,500 tigers in captivity around the world. Tigers have always been a great favorite with zoo visitors. One of the most popular kinds, the "white" tiger, has a creamy white coat with brownish black stripes. It is not really a different subspecies of tiger, but a mutation, or genetic change, seen especially with the Bengal tiger.

Tigers breed well in captivity. The Siberian tiger population has more individuals in captivity (about 660) than in the wild (200–300). In North America, tiger breeding programs are so successful that some females have been put on birth control.

In zoos around the world, the conservation of animals is becoming more and more important. Zoos are working with wildlife organizations to preserve endangered species. Because most tigers in the wild survive in small, isolated populations, they run the risk of dying out. Scientists are considering introducing some captive tigers back into the wild. Some worry that tigers who are used to being fed every day will never be able to hunt for themselves. Another alternative may be the artificial transplantation of sperm or embryos into wild tigers.

◊ Protecting the Tiger

The mysterious tiger has been a symbol of power and strength for centuries. Its power is a challenge to hunters, who have tried to kill it to prove their own skill and bravery. In India throughout the nineteenth and early twentieth centuries, large parties of sportsmen from around the world used to go out on huge tiger hunts. Hundreds of tigers could be killed in a few weeks. (The record was held by a maharaja of Surguja, who killed 1,100 in his lifetime.)

As a result of this overhunting, combined with loss of habitat, tiger populations plummeted. The population of tigers in India dropped from about 40,000 at the turn of the twentieth century to about 2,000 by 1972.

With the help of India and other concerned countries, The World Wildlife Fund founded Operation Tiger in 1972 to save the tiger from extinction. Since then, seventeen tiger reserves have been set up, and the tiger population in India has risen to between 4,000 and 5,000—the largest population of tigers in the world.

What about the other tiger subspecies? In 1987, there were approximately 1,000 Sumatran tigers, 2,000 or more Indo-Chinese tigers, 200–300 Siberian tigers, and fewer than 40 Chinese tigers left in the wild. Many countries have set up special reserves for their tigers. But the tiger's habitat continues to disappear.

Tigers live in still-developing countries, where people are poor and need land for their growing families. When tiger reserves were set aside in India, some people had to leave villages their ancestors had lived in for centuries. They were forbidden to graze their livestock or gather wood and brush in the forest.

Often people do not understand why the land they need for farms is set aside for tigers and other wildlife. Tigers, like

Operation Tiger sponsors research projects to study the tiger. Here a scientific team weighs a wild tiger that has been sedated.

people, are part of the web of life on this earth. Destroying the tiger's habitat means destroying the forests and other natural areas that help to conserve soil, water, and fresh air.

But when people live on the edge of the tiger preserves, tigers sometimes kill their livestock. Sometimes tigers attack people too—about 600 people in India have been killed by tigers in the last dozen years. Usually tigers do not eat humans. But old, wounded, and displaced tigers can become habitual maneaters.

In one area in India, villagers have come up with an ingenious solution. They wire lifelike human dummies to a battery so that the tigers get an electric shock when they attack. It is hoped that this way tigers will learn to avoid people.

But the conflict between human and tiger remains. Only if people have enough food, shelter, and fuel will the tiger survive in the long run. And only if the tiger and its forest survive will people have a natural world they can return to.

About the Contributors

JANE GOODALL was born in London on April 3, 1934, and grew up in Bournemouth, on the southern coast of England. In 1960, she began studying chimpanzees in the wild in Gombe, Tanzania. After receiving her doctorate in ethology at Cambridge University, Dr. Goodall founded the Gombe Stream Research Center for the study of chimpanzees and baboons. In 1977, she established the Jane Goodall Institute for Wildlife Research, Education and Conservation to promote animal research throughout the world. She has written three books for adults, including the bestseller *In the Shadow of Man*, and three books for children, including the acclaimed *My Life With the Chimpanzees* and *The Chimpanzee Family Book*.

RUTH ASHBY received her education at Yale College and the University of Virginia and has taught writing at UVA and Marymount Manhattan College. She edits science and wildlife books and is the author of two other books for children, Time Machine #23: *Quest for King Arthur*, and *Sea Otters*.

Jane Goodall's commitment to the animal world is expressed in her words, "Only when we understand can we care. Only when we care can we help. Only when we help shall they be saved." You can learn more about joining in her efforts to protect endangered wildlife by contacting The Jane Goodall Institute for Wildlife Research, Education and Conservation, P.O. Box 26846, Tucson, Arizona 85726.

Aladdin Books
Macmillan Publishing Company
866 Third Avenue, New York, NY 10022
Collier Macmillan Canada, Inc.

First Aladdin Books edition 1990

Printed in the United States of America

10 9 8 7 6 5 4 3 2 1

Interior illustrations by Ralph Reese

A hardcover edition of *Jane Goodall's Animal World: Tigers* is available from Atheneum Publishers, Macmillan Publishing Company.

10 9 8 7 6 5 4 3 2 1

Special thanks to Peter Jackson, Henry Blanke, Judy Wilson, Jonathan Lanman, and Ana Cerro.

Editor: Ruth Ashby
Associate Editor: Gillian Bucky
Cover design: Ted Mader & Associates
Interior design: Alex Jay/Studio J

Library of Congress Cataloging-in-Publication Data
Ashby, Ruth.
Jane Goodall's animal world. Tigers/by Ruth Ashby.
—1st Aladdin Books ed. p. cm.
"A Byron Preiss Book."
Summary: An introduction to tigers, beautiful solitary creatures of the Asian continent.
ISBN 0-689-71393-2
1. Tigers—Juvenile literature. [1. Tigers.] I. Title.
QL737.C23A84 1990b 599.74'428—dc20 89-78130